Torque brims with excitement perfect for thrill-seekers of all kinds. Discover daring survival skills, explore uncharted worlds, and marvel at mighty engines and extreme sports. In *Torque* books, anything can happen. Are you ready?

This edition first published in 2025 by Bellwether Media, Inc.

No part of this publication may be reproduced in whole or in part without written permission of the publisher. For information regarding permission, write to Bellwether Media, Inc., Attention: Permissions Department, 6012 Blue Circle Drive, Minnetonka, MN 55343.

Library of Congress Cataloging-in-Publication Data

LC record for Bundesliga available at: https://lccn.loc.gov/2024022427

Text copyright © 2025 by Bellwether Media, Inc. TORQUE and associated logos are trademarks and/or registered trademarks of Bellwether Media, Inc. Bellwether Media is a division of Chrysalis Education Group.

Editor: Kieran Downs   Designer: Gabriel Hilger

Printed in the United States of America, North Mankato, MN.

TABLE OF CONTENTS

BUNDESLIGA CHAMPIONS	4
WHAT IS THE BUNDESLIGA?	6
HISTORY OF THE BUNDESLIGA	8
THE BUNDESLIGA TODAY	12
FAST FACTS	20
GLOSSARY	22
TO LEARN MORE	23
INDEX	24

BUNDESLIGA CHAMPIONS

It is the last match day of the 2022–2023 Bundesliga season. Bayern Munich needs a win to be the Bundesliga **champions**. They score an early **goal** against Cologne. But the match stays close.

Cologne scores on a **penalty kick** with about 10 minutes to go. But with just over 1 minute left, Bayern scores. They have won the Bundesliga!

BAYERN MUNICH

STARS OF THE LEAGUE

Bayern's win in the 2022-2023 season was their 11th championship win in a row.

5

WHAT IS THE BUNDESLIGA?

The Bundesliga is the top level of **professional** soccer in Germany. There are 18 teams in the league each season. Players come from around the world to play for these teams.

The league is known for its fast-paced style of play. It is also known for the close ties between teams and their home communities.

THE 50+1 RULE

The league has a rule that teams must be mostly owned by members of the club. This helps keep fans happy and ticket prices low.

HISTORY OF THE BUNDESLIGA

Before the Bundesliga, soccer teams in Germany played in smaller **regional** leagues. After a disappointing **World Cup** in 1962, Germans wanted to see better players. They also wanted to keep their star players from playing in other leagues.

The first Bundesliga season began in 1963. The first 16 teams were chosen based on their play in the smaller leagues.

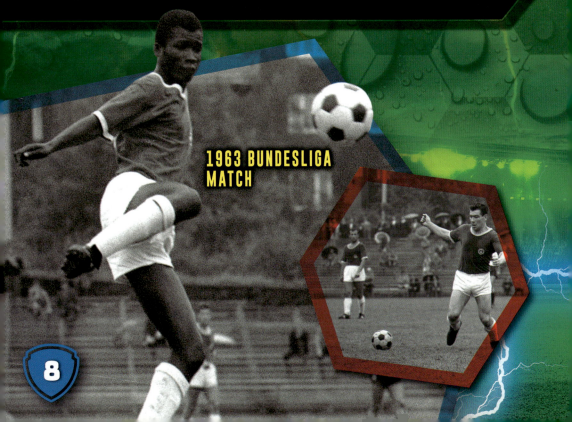

1963 BUNDESLIGA MATCH

FOUNDING TEAMS

- 1860 MUNICH
- BORUSSIA DORTMUND
- COLOGNE
- EINTRACHT BRAUNSCHWEIG
- EINTRACHT FRANKFURT
- HAMBURG
- HERTHA BERLIN
- KAISERSLAUTERN
- KARLSRUHE
- MSV DUISBURG
- NUREMBERG
- PREUßEN MUNSTER
- SAARBRÜCKEN
- SCHALKE
- VfB STUTTGART
- WERDER BREMEN

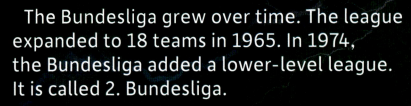

The Bundesliga grew over time. The league expanded to 18 teams in 1965. In 1974, the Bundesliga added a lower-level league. It is called 2. Bundesliga.

The league added **playoff** matches in 1981. These games decide which teams are **relegated** and **promoted** for the next season. In 1991, the league reached 20 teams. It returned to 18 in 1992.

1975 2. BUNDESLIGA MATCH

TIMELINE

1962
West Germany disappoints in the World Cup

1963
The first Bundesliga season begins with 16 teams

1965
The league adds two more teams

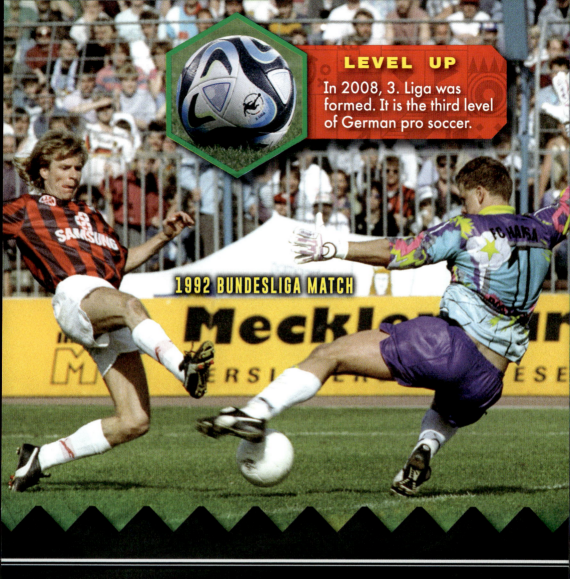

LEVEL UP

In 2008, 3. Liga was formed. It is the third level of German pro soccer.

1992 BUNDESLIGA MATCH

1974
2. Bundesliga is formed

1981
Promotion and relegation playoffs are added to the league

11

THE BUNDESLIGA TODAY

Each Bundesliga team plays 34 matches. The season usually begins in late August. Teams go on winter break around halfway through the season. Players have about a month off starting in mid-December.

The second half of the season begins in mid-January. The final match day is usually in May.

Teams earn points for how well they play in matches. Winning teams earn three points. Both teams get one point for a tie. Losing teams do not get any points.

The team with the most points at the end of the season wins the league. If teams are tied, the winner is decided by **goal difference**.

TOP PLAYERS

GERD MÜLLER

9 — FORWARD
Played for Bayern Munich, 1964–1979

FRANZ BECKENBAUER

5 — SWEEPER
Played for Bayern Munich, 1965–1977

BASTIAN SCHWEINSTEIGER

31 — CENTER BACK
Played for Bayern Munich, 2002–2015

MATS HUMMELS

15 — CENTER BACK
Played for Borussia Dortmund, 2007–2016, 2019–present

MANUEL NEUER

1 — GOALKEEPER
Played for Bayern Munich, 2011–present

At the end of the season, the two teams with the fewest points are relegated to 2. Bundesliga. The two top teams from 2. Bundesliga are promoted to the higher league.

The team in 16th place plays two playoff matches against the 3rd-place team from 2. Bundesliga. The team with the higher total score plays in the Bundesliga.

2023 PLAYOFF MATCH

RELEGATION AND PROMOTION

1. RELEGATION
The bottom two Bundesliga teams are relegated.

2. PROMOTION
The top two 2. Bundesliga teams are promoted.

3. PLAYOFFS
The 16th-place Bundesliga team plays two matches against the 3rd-place 2. Bundesliga team. The winner plays in the Bundesliga the next year.

2023 CHAMPIONS LEAGUE MATCH

The top four or five Bundesliga teams play in the **Champions League**. The next two teams get to play in the **Europa League**. These **tournaments** are against other top European teams.

18

Bundesliga fans love to cheer on their favorite teams. They sing songs and wear scarves to matches. Some even set off fireworks! There are many ways to enjoy Bundesliga soccer!

GERMAN CUP

Most pro soccer teams in Germany also play in the German Cup. The tournament features 64 teams.

FAST FACTS

NUMBER OF TEAMS | 18

YEAR STARTED | 1963

LARGEST STADIUM

SIGNAL IDUNA PARK
BORUSSIA DORTMUND

Capacity: about 81,365 people
Location: Dortmund, Germany

CLUB RECORDS
(AS OF 2023)

CLUBS WITH MOST APPEARANCES — **59 SEASONS**
FC BAYERN MUNICH AND SV WERDER BREMEN

CLUB WITH MOST CHAMPIONSHIPS — **32**
FC BAYERN MUNICH

FIRST CHAMPION
FC COLOGNE

CLUBS THAT HAVE PARTICIPATED IN THE LEAGUE — **57**

INDIVIDUAL RECORDS
(AS OF 2023)

Most career league goals
Gerd Müller: 365 goals

Most goals scored in a single season
Robert Lewandowski: 41 in 2020–2021

Fastest goals scored
Karim Bellarabi and Kevin Volland: 9 seconds

Person with most league appearances
Karl-Heinz Körbel: 602 appearances

GLOSSARY

champions—winners of a contest that decides the best team or person

Champions League—a European soccer tournament where the top teams of the top European leagues play each other to decide the best team in Europe

Europa League—a European soccer tournament for the next best teams that did not make the Champions League

goal—a score in soccer; a player scores a goal by sending the ball into the other team's net.

goal difference—the number of goals scored by a team minus the number of goals allowed by the team

penalty kick—a free kick awarded after a foul by an opponent within the penalty area

playoff—related to matches played after the regular season is over; playoff matches determine which team plays in the Bundesliga the next season.

professional—related to a player or team that makes money playing a sport

promoted—moved up to a higher league

regional—from a certain area in a country

relegated—moved down to a lower league

tournaments—series of matches in which several teams try to win the championship

World Cup—an international soccer competition held every four years; the World Cup is the world's largest soccer tournament.

TO LEARN MORE

AT THE LIBRARY

Bowman, Chris. *Premier League*. Minneapolis, Minn.: Bellwether Media, 2025.

Gish, Ashley. *La Liga*. Minneapolis, Minn.: Bellwether Media, 2025.

Goldblatt, David. *The Soccer Book: The Teams, the Rules, the Leagues, the Tactics*. New York, N.Y.: DK Publishing, 2021.

ON THE WEB

FACTSURFER

Factsurfer.com gives you a safe, fun way to find more information.

1. Go to www.factsurfer.com

2. Enter "Bundesliga" into the search box and click 🔍.

3. Select your book cover to see a list of related content.

INDEX

2. Bundesliga, 10, 16
3. Liga, 11
champions, 4, 5
Champions League, 18
Europa League, 18
fans, 7, 19
fast facts, 20–21
founding teams, 9
German Cup, 19
Germany, 6, 8, 11, 19
goal, 4
goal difference, 14
history, 4, 5, 8, 9, 10, 11
match, 4, 8, 10, 11, 12, 13, 14, 16, 18, 19
penalty kick, 4

players, 6, 8, 12, 15
playoff matches, 10, 16
points, 14, 16
promoted, 10, 16
relegated, 10, 16
relegation and promotion, 17
season, 4, 5, 6, 8, 10, 12, 13, 14, 16
style, 7
teams, 4, 5, 6, 7, 8, 9, 10, 12, 14, 16, 18, 19
timeline, 10–11
top players, 15
World Cup, 8

The images in this book are reproduced through the courtesy of: Matthias Schrader/ AP Images, cover, pp. 4, 4-5, 23; Vitalii Vitleo, p. 3; Marius Becker/ AP Images, p. 5 (stars of the league); imageBROKER.com GmbH & Co. KG/ Alamy, p. 6; Powerpics/ Alamy, pp. 7, 14; Moritz Müller/ Alamy, p. 7 (the 50+1 rule); Sven Simon/ picture-alliance/dpa/AP Images, pp. 8 (1963 Bundesliga match, inset), 10 (1963, 1965); Bundesliga/ Wiki Commons, pp. 9 (Bundesliga Team Logos), 17 (Bundesliga league logos), 20 (Bundesliga logo), 21 (FC Cologne); Werner Otto/ Alamy, pp. 10 (1975 2. Bundesliga match), 11 (1974, 1981), 21 (Kevin Volland); dpa picture alliance/ Alamy, pp. 10 (1962), 11 (level up), 15 (Gerd Müller), 19, 21 (Karim Bellarabi); Kai-Uwe Wärner/ picture-alliance/dpa/AP Images, p. 11 (1992 Bundesliga match); Phillip von Ditfurth/ AP Images, p. 12; Marius Becker/ picture-alliance/dpa/AP Images, p. 13; PA Images/ Alamy, pp. 15 (Franz Beckenbauer, Bastian Schweinsteiger), 21 (Gerd Müller, Karl-Heinz Körbel); Orange Pics BV/ Alamy, p. 15 (Mats Hummels); Aflo Co. Ltd./ Alamy, p. 15 (Manuel Neuer); Soeren Stache/ picture-alliance/dpa/AP Images, p. 16; Xinhua/ Alamy, p. 18; Andreas Gora/ AP Images, p. 19 (German cup); Tom Weller/ picture-alliance/dpa/AP Images, p. 20 (inset); Tupungato, p. 20 (Signal Iduna Park); Marcio Machado/ AP Images, p. 21 (Robert Lewandowski).